EASTER BUNNY CUTIES

A BOLD AND EASY EASTER COLORING BOOK

THIS BOOK BELONGS TO:

_____

EASTER BUNNY CUTIES: A BOLD AND EASY EASTER COLORING BOOK
Copyright © 2026 Dropthorn Press
All rights reserved.

No part of this book may be reproduced, stored in a retrieval system, or transmitted in any form or by any means — electronic, mechanical, photocopying, recording, or otherwise — without the prior written permission of the copyright owner.

ISBN: 978-1-970516-08-1
First Edition: 2026
Printed in the United States

10 9 8 7 6 5 4 3 2 1

TEST YOUR MARKER SET

PUT A PIECE OF PAPER UNDER YOUR PAGE WHILE COLORING SO IT DOESN'T BLEED THROUGH

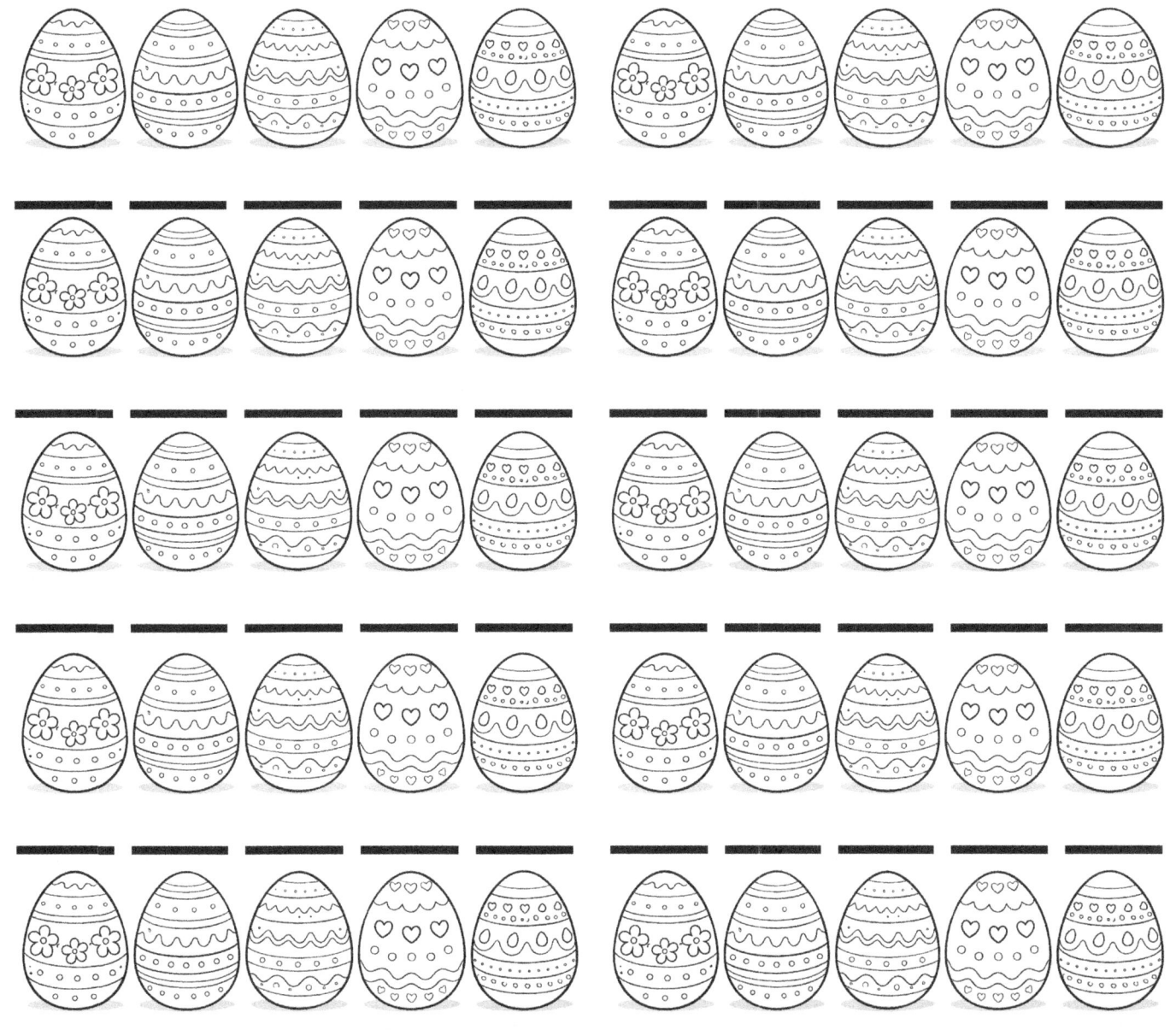

We hope that you enjoyed our book!

Check out other titles from Dropthorn Press:

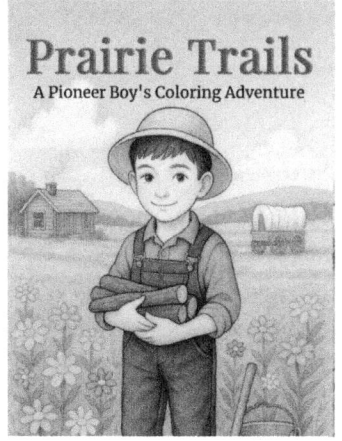
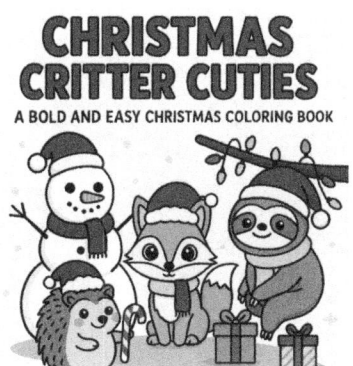

We hope that you enjoyed our book.

Made in the USA
Coppell, TX
23 January 2026